Contents

Welcome!

How many times a day do you feel unsure and think "I can't"? How many times do you feel confident and think "I can"?

Feeling unsure can make it hard to make friends, to fit into a new place, or to learn a new skill.

But if you believe in yourself, you can do almost anything!

Everyone feels unsure about themselves at times. Some people also find it hard to speak up in front of others.

This book is about how to feel confident and speak up. Read the stories and find out what other children do to help them say "I can."

About This Book

In every chapter, there are stories about children like you. Look out for the colored boxes.

Each story has a different color. Find out how each person deals with the same kind of worries you may have.

Every chapter also gives examples of other feelings and situations that make people feel unsure.

At the end of each chapter find out how the people in the stories cope with their feelings.

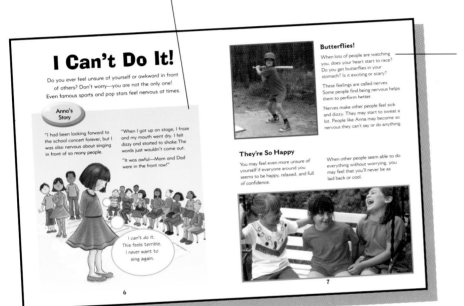

Learn ways to deal with difficult feelings or situations.

Turn to the back for tips on how to feel more confident and for lists of helpful books, Web sites, and addresses.

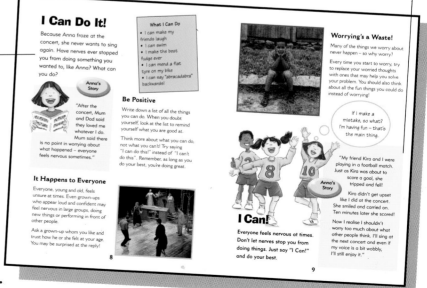

I Can't Do It!

Do you ever feel unsure of yourself or awkward in front of others? Don't worry—you are not the only one! Even famous sports and pop stars feel nervous at times.

Anna's Story

"I had been looking forward to the school concert forever, but I was also nervous about singing in front of so many people.

"When I got up on stage, I froze and my mouth went dry. I felt dizzy and started to shake. The words just wouldn't come out.

"It was awful—Mom and Dad were in the front row!"

I can't do it. This feels terrible. I never want to sing again.

Butterflies!

When lots of people are watching you, does your heart start to race? Do you get butterflies in your stomach? Is it exciting or scary?

These feelings are called nerves. Some people find being nervous helps them to perform better.

Nerves make other people feel sick and dizzy. They may start to sweat a lot. People like Anna may become so nervous they can't say or do anything.

They're So Happy

You may feel even more unsure of yourself if everyone around you seems to be happy, relaxed, and full of confidence.

When other people seem able to do everything without worrying, you may feel that you'll never be as laid back or cool.

I Can Do It!

Because Anna froze at the concert, she never wants to sing again. Have nerves ever stopped you from doing something you wanted to, like Anna? What can you do?

Anna's Story

"After the concert, Mom and Dad said they loved me whatever I do. Mom said there is no point in worrying about what happened—everyone feels nervous sometimes."

It Happens to Everyone

Everyone, young and old, feels unsure at times. Even grown-ups who act loud and confident may feel nervous in large groups, doing new things, or performing in front of other people.

Ask a grown-up whom you like and trust how he or she felt at your age. You may be surprised at the reply!

What I Can Do

- I can make my friends laugh
- I can swim
- I make the best fudge ever
- I can fix a flat tire on my bike
- I can say "abracadabra" backward!

Be Positive

Make a list of all the things you can do. When you doubt yourself, look at the list to remind yourself what you are good at.

Think more about what you can do, not what you can't! Try saying "I can do this!" instead of "I can't do this." Remember, as long as you do your best, you're doing great.

Worrying's a Waste!

Many of the things we worry about never happen—so why worry?

Every time you start to worry, try to replace your worried thoughts with ones that may help you solve your problem. You should also think about all the fun things you could do instead of worrying!

If I make a mistake, so what? I'm having fun—that's the main thing.

Anna's Story

"My friend Kira and I were playing in a soccer match. Just as Kira was about to score a goal, she tripped and fell!

"Kira didn't get upset like I did at the concert. She smiled and went on. Ten minutes later, she scored!

"Now I realize I shouldn't worry too much about what other people think. I'll sing at the next concert and even if my voice is a little shaky, I'll still enjoy it."

I Can!

Everyone feels nervous at times. Don't let nerves stop you from doing things. Just say "I can!" and do your best.

I Feel Left Out

Do you find it easy to make friends or does it feel really hard? Some people love being in large groups, but others can find it difficult to join in.

I wish I could be like them. They're all having such fun.

Carl's Story

"My cousin Ben invited me to his birthday party, but he was the only person I knew there. The other kids all knew each other. I felt so left out.

"A boy came up and spoke to me. I was so shy. I didn't know what to say, even though I wanted to talk. Then he walked off. I hate being like this."

Pick Me!

Have you ever been left until last when your class gets into teams or pairs?

Do you feel hurt and embarrassed and think that you have been deliberately left until last? Or do you say to yourself, "Okay, today it's my turn to be picked last. I'll just do my best for my team!"?

No One to Play With

Look around at recess. Does anyone look left out?

It is good to be alone sometimes, but some children hate recess because they don't have friends. They may be alone, watching everyone else have fun. Even though they'd love to join in with others, they may feel scared inside.

Feeling Alone

You may want to be invited over to someone's house or to play in the park—but no one asks.

Perhaps you recently moved. You don't know anyone and you feel unsure about meeting new people. This can make you feel lonely.

Join In!

Carl is upset because he would like to join in, but he isn't sure how. Carl may worry less if he realizes that lots of people are quiet like he is. Can you think of anything else to help Carl join in?

Carl's Story

"Dad said that sometimes he finds it hard to join in, too. But it's OK. It gives him time to see what's going on and to see who he'd like to talk to. He takes deep breaths to help him relax."

Ask Them

You can make the first move toward making a new friend. Ask your parents or sitter if you can invite someone over to play, or if you can have a party.

If you notice someone is lonely, try to include him or her in your games. It will mean a lot to that person.

You Choose

In team sports, everyone wants to be chosen by someone. So why not choose a partner first? Someone else probably wants to be picked, too.

If you are the person picked last, remember that it will be someone else's turn next time. Above all, don't let it spoil the game for you. In time, you will make friends who will be eager to pick you as a partner.

Practice Makes Perfect

Learning to ride a bicycle takes time and practice. At first, you wobble or even fall off. After a while, it's easy!

Making friends takes practice too. Talk to a parent or sitter about how to get involved with others at recess. You could start by talking to someone new each day, even if it's just a simple "Hi."

This is fun! I think she likes me.

I Can!

Think to yourself: "I'll take my time, look friendly, and choose the person I'll talk to. When I speak up, it is easier to join in. I can make friends."

Carl's Story

"Before I went to another party, I thought about things I could talk about. I took my time and made an effort not to look uncomfortable. I kept my head up and smiled.

"Then I saw this girl. She looked friendly. It felt very scary walking up to her, but once I started, I was OK. I still felt a bit nervous, but I had a great time."

I Feel Different

We are all different, from the way we look to the hobbies we enjoy. That's what makes each one of us special. But sometimes other people make us feel uncomfortable about the things that make us different.

Emma's Story

"I hate having to wear glasses! Some kids on my street tease me about them. They call me names and say mean things to me. Nobody else I know has to wear them. I don't want anyone to see me because I feel so embarrassed.

"I used to enjoy going to the playground, but I'm scared everyone there will laugh at me as well. I don't know what to do!"

It's not fair. Why *do* I have to wear glasses?

Avoiding the Crowd

It's good to be on your own sometimes. But a few children feel so uncomfortable about being with others that they spend most of their time alone, watching TV or playing computer games.

The fear of being with others can make a person feel lonely and distant from everyone else.

With Grown-ups

Some children find it hard to make friends in a group of other children. They may prefer being with grown-ups, such as grandparents, instead of other children. This may make them feel safer.

Oh No!

Has one of your parents or sitters talked loudly about you in front of lots of people so everyone turns to stare at you? Perhaps one of them dresses or behaves in a way that makes you cringe.

Feeling so embarrassed about what someone else says or does can make you want to disappear!

Look at Me!

Throughout your life, there will be lots of times when people want to hear what you have to say. Even if it makes you a bit nervous, speaking out helps you to join in.

Shiv's Story

"I started sitting at the back of the room and skipped some classes. My teacher asked me what was going on. I told her I hated speaking up in class.

"She said she used to be nervous in front of a class, but that there are things you can do to help. Great!"

A Kids' World

It is great spending time with older brothers and sisters or grandparents, but it is also important to be with children of your own age.

It can feel safer being with grown-ups because they take charge, but playing with other children can be a lot of fun!

Give It a Try

Avoiding other children makes you feel lonely. But joining in can make you feel good and helps you to feel that you belong. Every day, try to join in with an activity. Soon you will be playing with friends!

Try Again

If someone is always left out, why not ask him or her to play? At first, he or she may say no, but it is worth asking again. Some people may need a bit of encouragement!

That's How They Are!

All parents do things that may embarrass us, but it's important to understand that everyone is different. We can't ask our parents to change just so they don't embarrass us, but we can gently let them know how we feel.

Try to enjoy the people you love for who they are, instead of worrying about what others may think.

I Can!

If you find it hard to speak up, say to yourself: "Take a deep breath, relax my body, hold my head high, and go for it. I can do it!"

Wow... I could get used to all this attention.

"My teacher said it helps to think about what I want to say before I speak, or even to write a few notes to myself if I need to. Now I take some slow, deep breaths before speaking up, and I don't worry about taking my time.

"I've also joined the drama club, where I can practice speaking in front of a group. I've made a couple of new friends, too."

Shiv's Story

21

I Give Up!

In life there are lots of exciting things to learn and experience. At times they can be difficult and frustrating. But you can stay confident even when things are hard.

Ina's Story

"Last night I was doing my math homework in the kitchen and I got really fed up.

"I hate math. It's too hard and I can't do it. Everyone else I know finds it easy.

"I'm also tired of being told that my brother is brilliant at math.

"I feel useless. There's no point in trying anymore."

This is a stupid subject!

Never Good Enough

Do you ever try really hard at a task to please someone you care about—but he or she only finds fault with it? Perhaps you did the dishes, but your dad only noticed the cup you forgot.

This can make you believe that you'll never be able to do anything right.

In the Shade

Is your brother or sister good at everything? Perhaps your best friend is the most popular person at school and great at sports?

If you think you are only second-best, you may feel worthless and even less loved than someone else. You may feel as if you will never be as successful as the other person—so there is no point in trying.

Why Bother?

Being enthusiastic or making an effort is a positive, exciting feeling.

But if no one seems to notice your efforts, you may just want to give up and not bother.

Do My Best

Feeling that you're no good at something makes it even harder. Don't give up! Take your time, think about the things you are good at, and try again!

Ina's Story

"I talked to Mom. She said it doesn't matter if I'm not great at math like my brother. What matters is that I do my best and enjoy the things that I am good at."

Listen to Praise

It's not easy to feel confident if someone important to you, such as your Mom, Dad or sitter, seems to only criticize you.

Try to remember the compliments that other people, such as teachers and friends, give you. When people do praise you, trust what they say. Treasure their words of praise for the times when you feel low.

Give Yourself Time

You have lots of time to learn and lots of different things to do—so be easy on yourself when something is hard.

If you want to do something but find it difficult, start with a simple task before trying something hard. If playing soccer drives you crazy because you keep missing the ball, take some time to practice with a friend!

24

Listen to Advice

If someone criticizes your efforts, you may feel upset. When you feel calmer, think about what the person said.

Was she or he trying to show you a different way of doing something, rather than just criticizing you? Is it his or her way of trying to help you?

I Can!

Say to yourself: "I can listen to helpful advice. I can be positive and try again. I can ask someone for help. If I do my best, then that's fine. There are lots of things I can do."

It's not easy, but I understand it better now.

Ina's Story

"I'm enjoying the things I can do instead of trying to compare myself to my brother. We're different, that's all.

"Mom talked to my teachers at school. I'm going to get more help with math. It's still hard, but I'm not going to give up. Now I know that when I find one thing hard, it doesn't mean that I'm useless."

All Change

Starting new things or meeting new people can be hard for anyone, even outgoing people. It can feel especially difficult if you feel quiet or unsure about yourself.

Pavel looks so sad. I feel really sorry for him.

"Last week this new boy called Pavel joined our school. He's from another country, and he doesn't know anyone.

"I feel sorry for him. He's quiet and nobody talks to him.

"My friends don't want him to play with us.

"I think it's mean, but I don't want to argue with them."

May's Story

New Faces

It is not always easy meeting new people at family gatherings or celebrations. If you move, you will meet new neighbors.

Some grown-ups can be very embarrassing when they meet you for the first time. They might say, "My, you're shy!" or "Haven't you got any friends?"

This Feels Wrong

Have you ever been asked to say or do something that you don't agree with, such as being mean to someone? Perhaps somebody tried to stop you from playing with someone else.

Some people find it easy to stand up for themselves and say, "No." Others find it hard and end up doing something they know is wrong, like being mean to a new boy or girl at school.

Moving On

It can be hard to say goodbye to the people and places that you know well. If you move to a new school, you may miss your old classmates. If a favorite teacher leaves, you may worry that you won't get along as well with the new teacher.

Good Times!

May realizes Pavel finds the change in his life hard. She is not sure about asking Pavel to play. If you are in a situation like this, trust your feelings, and do what you feel is right and kind.

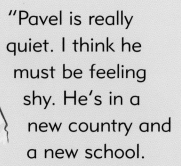

"Pavel is really quiet. I think he must be feeling shy. He's in a new country and a new school. I thought about how he must feel. I decided to ask Pavel to join in our game. He was so happy to be asked."

May's Story

Speak Up!

Before you meet new people, think of things to say that will help you feel more confident. If someone says that you are shy or quiet, you could reply, "I just take my time until I feel comfortable." It will help you feel bold and brave.

A New Choice

If you feel uncomfortable with something, do something about it. Speak up if a situation makes you unhappy. You have a right to choose your own friends.

If other people have a problem with this, they are not worth your time and effort. You can choose some new and better friends.

It's Exciting!

Life would be very dull if nothing ever changed. As you grow up, lots of things change. Some feel good, and others less so.

In time, you'll feel more secure and safe in new situations or with new people. Then the new things won't seem so strange.

I'm so glad I asked Pavel to join in. He's so funny!

"At first Pavel was really quiet and unsure. But he soon relaxed. Now he's used to the school and all the new things around him.

"Some of my friends were unfriendly to him, but the rest of us ignored them.

"Pavel's really OK. I'm glad I got to know him. He tells us some great jokes and makes some funny faces!"

May's Story

I Can!

Change can be an exciting adventure for me to enjoy. It may feel scary at first, but I can do it. I can enjoy it, too!

Remember

When you feel unsure of yourself, try to think of these tips. They can help you feel more confident.

• Just telling someone how you feel can make a problem or worry seem much less worrisome, and can make you feel better. It can also make the worries seem less important.

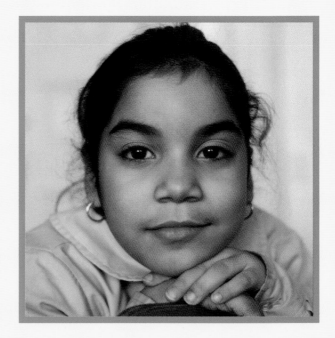

• Talk to friends, family, and teachers—that's what they are there for!

• If you have lots of worries on your mind, make a list of them and "empty" them from your mind. That way, they won't keep taking up so much space in your mind.

• Don't avoid doing things just because doing them makes you a little nervous. Fears go away when you start to face them and deal with them.

• Give it a try—it won't be as bad as you think!

Read About It

You can also look in your library or bookstore for books like these, which discuss the different feelings you may have:

Looking After Myself by Sarah Levete (1997)
A book about self-confidence and looking after yourself.

The Brand New Kid by Katie Couric (2000)
A story about what it is like to go to a new school.

Fears, Doubts, Blues, and Pouts by H. Norman Wright et al (1999)
A book of stories about dealing with fear, worry, sadness, and anger.

On the Web

These Web sites are also helpful:
www.childanxiety.net
www.kidshealth.org
www.bbc.co.uk/health/kids
www.think-positive.org.uk
www.keepkidshealthy.com
www.youngminds.org.uk

Extra help

If you need to talk to someone who doesn't know you, these organizations can help put you in touch with people trained to help:

Committee For Children
568 First Avenue South
Suite 600
Seattle
WA 98104-2804
Tel: 800-634-4449
Fax: 206-438-6765

The Center for Anxiety
and Related Disorders
at Boston University
648 Beacon Street
6th floor, Boston
MA 02215
Tel: 617-353-9610

National Mental Health
Association
1021 Prince Street
Alexandria
VA 22314-2971
Tel: 703-684-7722
Fax: 703-684-5968

Index

Photo credits

Abbreviations: t—top, m—middle, b—bottom, r—right, l—left, c—center. All pictures supplied by Corbis except for 1, 11ml, 11br, 12, 15tl, 17tl, 19mr, 19bl, 20t, 21, 23tl, 23mr, 27tl, 28tr, 31ml—Select Pictures. 7 both, 20br, 25mr—Digital Stock. 8—Ros Kavanagh.

All photographs in this book were posed by models.

The publishers would like to thank them all.